THE LAST RUNNERS
by
Virginie Beauregard D.

translated by

Peter Schulman

Finishing Line Press
Georgetown, Kentucky

THE LAST RUNNERS

Copyright © 2023 by Virginie Beauregard D. and Peter Schulman (Translator)
ISBN 979-8-88838-079-6 First Edition
All rights reserved under International and Pan-American Copyright Conventions.
No part of this book may be reproduced in any manner whatsoever without written
permission from the publisher, except in the case of brief quotations embodied in
critical articles and reviews.

ACKNOWLEDGMENTS

Many thanks to Carl Bessette and Jean-Sébastien Larouche at Les Editions
de l'Ecrou, the publishers of the *Les Derniers coureurs*, for their enthusiasm
and kind permission for this translation.

Publisher: Leah Huete de Maines
Editor: Christen Kincaid
Cover Art: Peter Schulman
Author Photo: Virginie Beauregard D.
Translator Photo: Muriel Singer
Cover Design: Elizabeth Maines McCleavy

Order online: www.finishinglinepress.com
              also available on amazon.com

Author inquiries and mail orders:
Finishing Line Press
P. O. Box 1626
Georgetown, Kentucky 40324
U. S. A.

Breathing in the crisp, bracing, early-morning air, I felt once again the joy of running on familiar ground

Haruki Murakami

to wake you so I could show you

the electric colors

of the very moment I robbed you

you fall
from your bed

as I part
with sleep

returning from an ordeal of secret trails

it did not seem like much

you flapped your feet as others would wings

it begs the question
are we those out of breath athletes
the ones who run in packs

on the sparkling eclipse
minutes and seasons
in a stadium that can barely recognize them

we jump into the crowd

a cloud

of dust and ash

meticulously

violence rests

on the trophies of our days

focused on
the last runners'
headbands

we revive
the enduring
embers

once the fire has taken

to its beat
mouths wide open we near
the territory's rapacious fold

already
the red sun tilts
the trees' silhouettes
and folds the sand

as a lung
might saturate
the unconscious colors of the shore

It seems as though the wind
were a golden rock
at the bottom of a nomad's satchel

it transforms
your garment
into a giant sail

So I tug at your sleeve
we should move towards the surface of things
searching
for a few traces of light

the heat that
grabs the rocky gravel
by both hands

the morning's orangy filter that
leans against a sky
I do not recognize

make me doubt that the stable lines
of no-return
are out there somewhere

I am on a voyage

an act

of tourism

I depend on the tired steps of a gray horse
while our veins
vacillate within nature

a path lays at the window of an appreciative silence
that extends all the way to a child's jawline
masticating its slumber

life stretches out
and beauty seemingly wants to grow
until its last stop

we fall into a trap
let us go towards what we need
to live and to die

by making the falcons
descend
into the swamps of our eyes

we will eventually
find
what we need to fly

we would have to take an inventory of winter
its magnetic force
I forget about during the course of a year

perhaps we should disguise
our strides upon the cold
as vast blue creatures

the dense forest
flexes its muscles
upon our approach

I stumble
into
a wet
rock

to replace you
by anything at all
a bear or an eyelash with black markings

that coyote
managing to distract me
from our presence

in the burning vessel of a forty-second kilometer
I attain the flesh
the scales
or something better

maybe a drumbeat of
obscure languages
or a diver's held breath

lively cartilage
one leg balances emptiness
the other fullness

moods
deep enough to reach
the blind fish

panic stricken
I regain the reach
of your boat-like eyes

in the jaws of strangulation
the world's
bestiaries

the lichen
continues to grow
beneath the snow from my distracted hands

it reminds me of prehistory
a pleasing thought
I stay

to advance perhaps

for now
I dance on the world's
vertebrae
with no complaints

people
are banded
animals

or forests
of just one tree
I am not sure

I see birds in mid-flight
depicting the sky
as they light themselves up from the earth

I laugh as I cry
but not in an ugly way
it is just the principle
of day and night

the obese day begins
with a bit of oil at the edge of our lips
and the allotment of luck that one needs
to stay alive

we redefine simple words
tell us which rocks
we should not step on

just athletic enough
to bypass reality
or to practice our wrestling

like idiots
we eliminate the harvest
and survival

to roll
through the city's
straw

in order to store
the radiance
of things

we gather our speed

in random time zones

determined to lose the star

frozen
between two faithless futures
we make our way through the flat wind

towards a satellite
left behind by giant
debris that incite us to deviate

as others
before us
we use the millennium as our excuse

so we act
like ecumenical gorillas
who yawn to show off their canine fangs

let us sweep our out of control world away

an orchestra magnifies the unfathomable
the deconstruction has already come to pass
in a powerful manner

we will comprehend the erosion
by jogging
on the gravel of every wind

our laughter pierces
the darkness'
brain

the tide
flows
into the blaze

we will not cease
to practice

tracing
flashes

far from the accident
I pick borders

along that big path
where what ifs cannot be compared

we jump up and down
on the mattress of the world
we are reassigned numbers

the riot breaks out
the windowpane a comet
within a misunderstood sky

the night is pushed to the brink of its predilection for metal
when you hear that the sky
builds upon shady recommendations

you wonder how
one can acclimate
to the in-between-hours

it's pitch -dark and once there
I have trouble making out
accents and voices

listening to music: yes
I'm not good at distinguishing
truth from falsehood

you slide the moon
to the bottom of
poorly recognized smiles

dropping invitations
like the sickly ash tree
disperses its leaves

I remain on my perch
inquiring about the weather to
the ones who live in other centuries

the ones who discover their image
in a puddle

here the drizzle papers
the lining of our coats
with ephemeral jewels

I weaken
the pearls
by my reach

the clock
persists
with inverted arms

we know no peace

all that is left for us to do now
is to watch the champions
go by and to salute them

women
towed by all their paraphernalia
limp their way towards the clouds

so that rain will fall
as well as this two- year old child

you return a queen's necklaces
then you extinguish

the evening's setting
beneath the opal of another city

on a seesaw
in a garden
of light

the child

fell
between two
employees of the State

as we feebly
turned our heads
we saw the wings

of such incredibly small
birds
flapping in the air

the birth
is taking longer
than expected

our hopes are focused
on some peak
reduced to a hill

your heart is still there
I remain
in an invisible rowboat

repeating to myself
that the minutes are born to fall
like the akenes in June

we will come up with
an idea
to get back to speed

and decant
the weight
of hours

our fingers
persevere
and fade away

we brush against
the shoulder of pleasure

there is work to be done
we have to polish
those wicked waves

one after the other

to help us
float

I find the river

by placing my hand

on your hip

skin

is the modest refuge

that I do not want to abandon

desire strays

in its construction site

of eccentricities

in order for the morning to function

we return
what we have already taken
from the light

the horizon embroiders
a ship
far from the coast

that will take in the waves
of your hesitations
one by one

engaged
by cormorants
the day's mobile axis

settles
at insomnia's
bedside

I witness the birth
of a drawing
with a double meaning

from another era
across your face

while the traces of my fatigue
slice up the grimaces of mortality
in the morning mirror

just as the wind
the snowdrifts
of February

soon
our pupils
will adopt

all forms
suitable
to mountains

with the juvenile finger we are left with
we will transcribe
the letters attached
to the foam

what is left of the sun
in the fjord of cribs
and ashes
and useless toys

because resetting the locks of the world
is within our jurisdiction

the beginnings of a new kind of archeology
hinge on the obvious
a dandelion root

you seek a dream
for the coming
nights

here it is

a horse
rolling
through the snow

the miracle

could well be

a latitude

one borrows

was it my idea
to draw
one of your drops of sweat

did I come up with
that slug
at the tip of your boot

I've fallen for a landscape
on the curve

counting the dust
that separates us
from the next day

Virginie Beauregard D. is the author of three acclaimed books of poetry: *Les heures se trompent de but (The hours miss their mark)* in 2010; in 2014 she published *D'une main sauvage (From a Savage Hand)* which was a finalist for the Emile Nelligan Prize in 2015 and a winner of the Jean Lafrenière Prize at the International Poetry Festival of Trois-Rivières in 2016. *Les derniers coureurs (The Last Runners)* in 2018 and was a finalist for the prestigious Prix des Libraires in 2019. All three volumes were published by Les Editions de l'Ecrou. In 2019, she published a children's book, *Perruche* (Parakeet) at *La Courte Echelle*. She is very active in the contemporary Quebecois poetry world and one of her earliest poems, *"Vous êtes tous des petits garçons qui rêvez de lilas en fleurs"* ("You are all little boys who dream of flowery lilacs") was performed by the theater company Théâtre de Quatre Sous in Montreal in 2009.

Dr. Peter Schulman is Professor of French and International Studies at Old Dominion University. He is the author of *The Sunday of Fiction: The Modern French Eccentric* (Purdue UP, 2003) as well as *Le Dernier Livre du Siècle* (Romillat, 2001) with Mischa Zabotin. He has translated Jules Verne's last novel *The Secret of Wilhelm Storitz*; George Simenon's *The 13 Culprits* as well as a meditation on waves by Marie Darrieussecq, *On Waves*; *Suburban Beauty* from poet Jacques Reda; *Adamah* from poet Celine Zins; Ying Chen's collection of haiku *Impressions of Summer* and Silvia Baron Supervielle's *Pages of Travel* . He is currently co-editor in chief of a journal of eco-criticism, *Green Humanities* with Josh Weinstein and has co-edited the following books: *The Marketing of Eros: Performance, Sexuality and Consumer Culture* (2003) ; *Chasing Esther: Jewish Expressions of Cultural Difference* (Kol Katan Press, 2006) and *Rhine Crossings: France and German in Love and War* (SUNY Press, 2005). His translation of Marie Nimier's play *Another Year, Another Christmas (Noel revient tous les ans)* was performed by the Haberdasher Theater company in Columbus Ohio and New York City in November 2017.

www.ingramcontent.com/pod-product-compliance
Lightning Source LLC
Chambersburg PA
CBHW030225170426
43194CB00007BA/866